Dragons

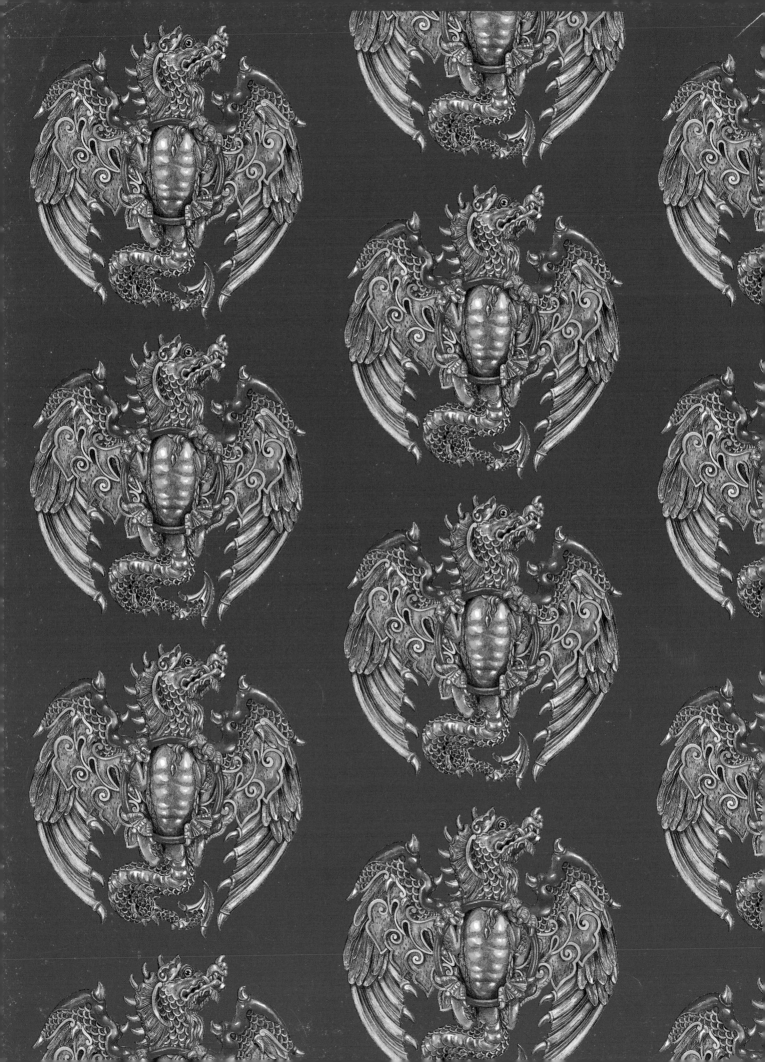

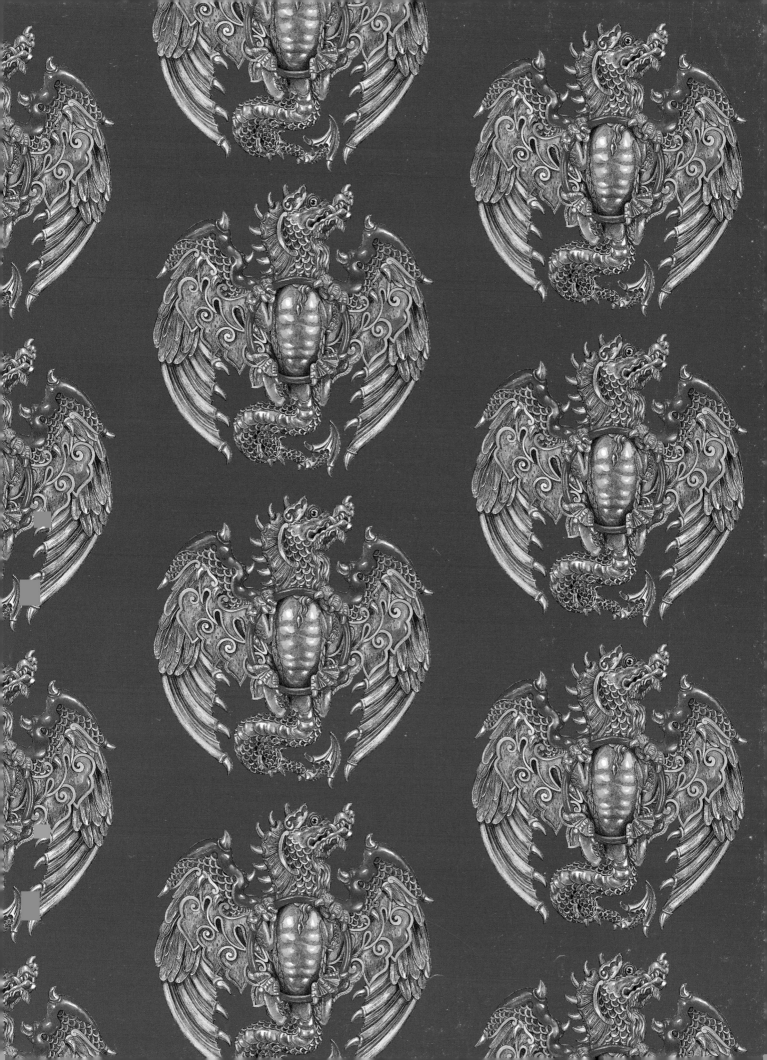

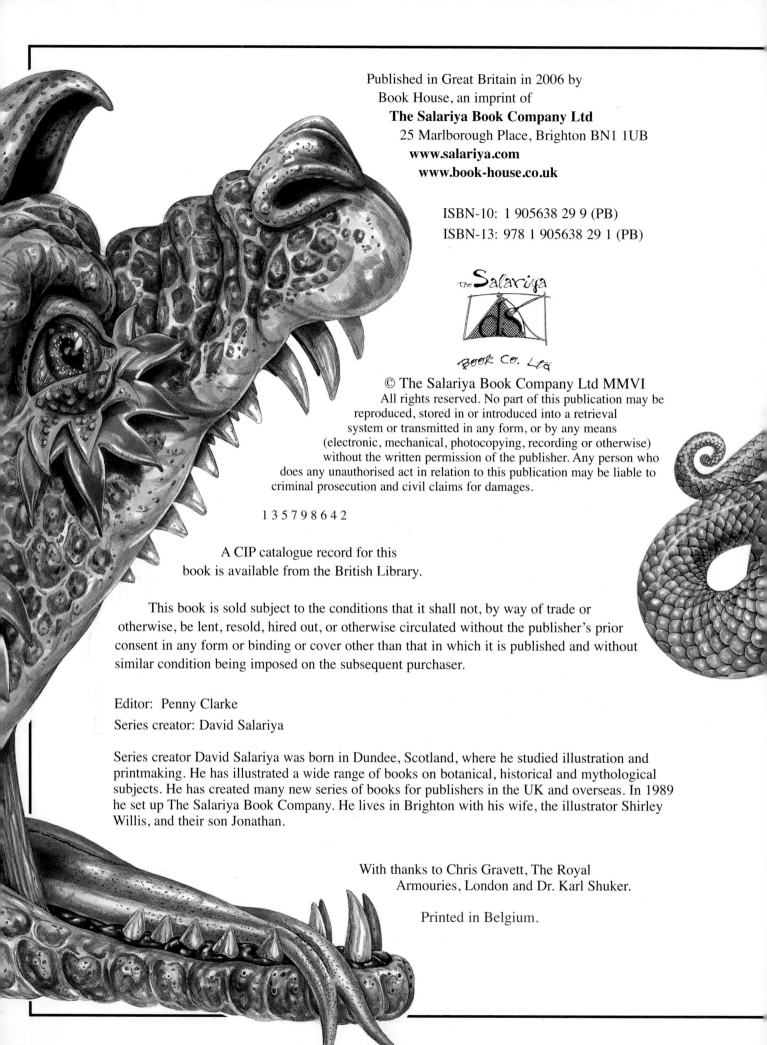

Published in Great Britain in 2006 by
Book House, an imprint of
The Salariya Book Company Ltd
25 Marlborough Place, Brighton BN1 1UB
www.salariya.com
www.book-house.co.uk

ISBN-10: 1 905638 29 9 (PB)
ISBN-13: 978 1 905638 29 1 (PB)

1 3 5 7 9 8 6 4 2

A CIP catalogue record for this
book is available from the British Library.

Editor: Penny Clarke

Series creator: David Salariya

Series creator David Salariya was born in Dundee, Scotland, where he studied illustration and
printmaking. He has illustrated a wide range of books on botanical, historical and mythological
subjects. He has created many new series of books for publishers in the UK and overseas. In 1989
he set up The Salariya Book Company. He lives in Brighton with his wife, the illustrator Shirley
Willis, and their son Jonathan.

With thanks to Chris Gravett, The Royal
Armouries, London and Dr. Karl Shuker.

Printed in Belgium.

Dragons

Written by
Gerald Legg

Illustrated by
Carolyn Scrace

Created and designed by
David Salariya

BOOK HOUSE

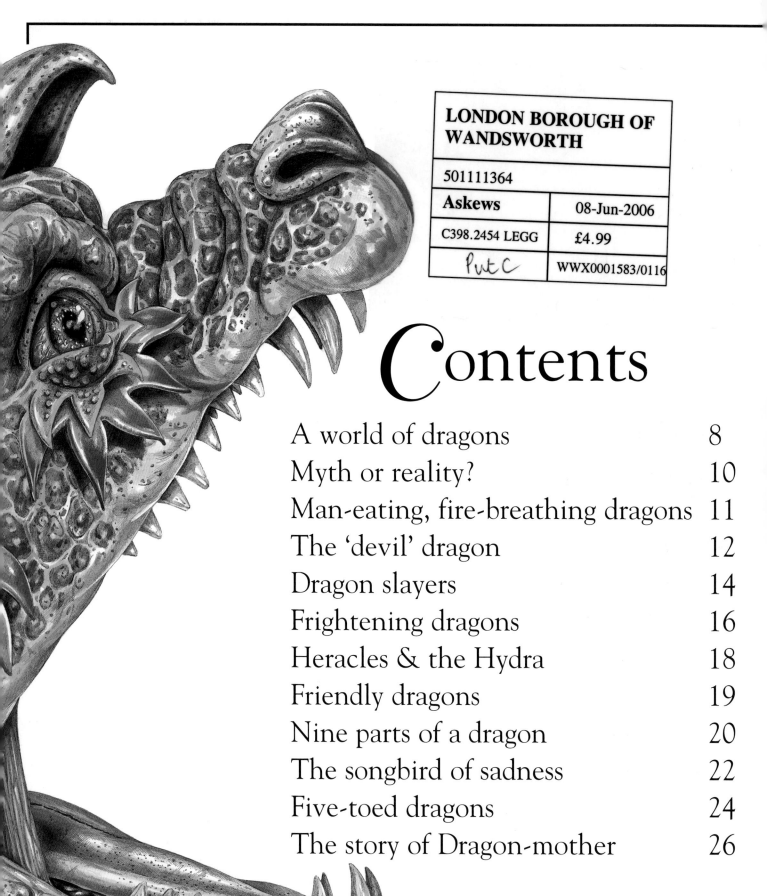

Contents

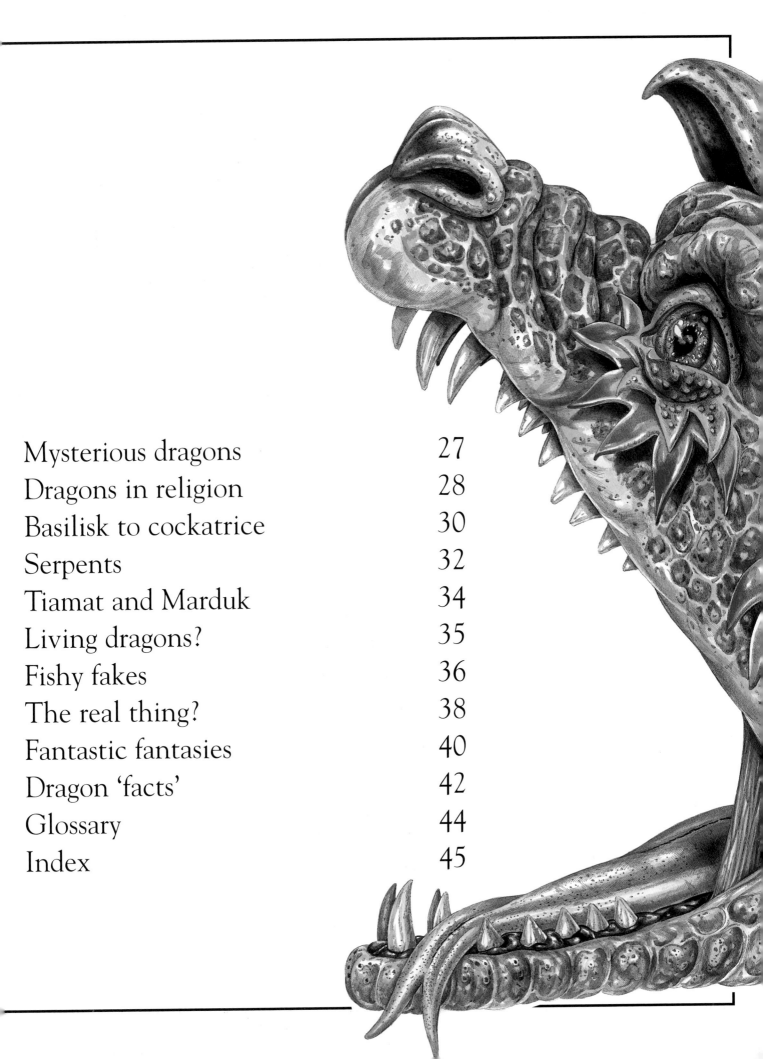

A world of dragons

In Canada, a huge serpent dragon rather like a whale lived in Lake Okanagan. It was called Ogopogo.

In Maine, Wewilmekq, a giant leech, bravely overcame a huge serpent, while in Illinois, the great dragon-bird Piasa was slain by a warrior of the Illlini people.

Quetzalcoatl was the Aztecs' and Toltecs' magnificently feathered snake-god of wisdom and life.

Stories about dragons occur everywhere in the world. All civilizations and cultures have legends involving these powerful and awe-inspiring mythological creatures. Most stories about dragons refer to their fire-breathing abilities. These probably refer back to memories of thunder and lightning or erupting volcanoes spewing fire into the sky. But while the dragons of the west are usually described as cruel, evil creatures, those of the east are often said to be kind and gentle. God-like in their powers, they are linked with the creation of the world, wisdom and knowledge.

Dragons of the world

1 **Canada** Serpent dragons and giant dragon whales.
2 **USA** Serpent dragons and serpent whales. Wewilmekq the giant leech and the Piasa dragon-bird.
3 **Mexico and Guatemala** Quetzalcoatl.
4 **West Indies** The crowing crested-cobra.
5 **Chile** The cockatrice of Lake Fagua.
6 **Scandinavia** Jormungander, the Midgard serpent. Fafnir and other serpent dragons.
7 **Iceland** The basilisk.

8 **Scotland** The Loch Ness Monster.
9 **Wales** Winged serpent dragons.
10 **Ireland** Sea lizards.
11 **England** The Lambton worm. Winged serpents and the Mordiford wyvern.
12 **Germany, Austria and Switzerland** The tatzelworm, the lindorm and the dragonet of Mount Pilatus.
13 **France** The Peluda, the Tarasque, salamanders and gargouilles.
14 **Italy** The tatzelworm and the dragon Typhon.

15 **Greece** The dragon of Poseidon, Scylla, the Hydra, salamanders and Python.
16 **Egypt** Mertseger and amphiteres.
17 **North Africa** The Carthaginian serpent and the dragon of Silene.
18 **Central Africa** Mokele-mbembe, the crowing-crested cobra.
19 **Ethiopia** The dragon of Silene.
20 **The Middle East** Leviathan and Tiamat, Sirrush, salamanders and amphiteres.

Many Norse myths describe a huge dragon-serpent that encircled and supported the earth.

There were many dragons in Greek mythology: the dragon of Poseidon, the sea god, the salamander which emerged from fire, and the dragon Python, a son of the earth killed by Apollo.

Mokele-mbembe roamed the swamps of the Congo.

The Middle East was rich in dragons: Leviathan, Sirrush and many lesser local ones, like salamanders. Further south, in Ethiopia, lived the dragon of Silene.

Although the lizard-like naga dragons of India were fierce, they were not as hostile to humans as their cousins in the west.

A real dragon lives in Indonesia: the Komodo dragon, at 3.7 metres, is the world's largest lizard. Only discovered in 1912 it could be the source of many local dragon legends.

The dragons of China, Japan and other parts of South-East Asia were noted for their friendliness towards humans.

In Australia the Bunyip lived in a swamp.

21 **India** Nagas, Ananta, Vritra and Makara.
22 **Indonesia** Komodo dragons.
23 **China** Imperial dragons and friendly dragons.

24 **Japan** The tatsu and O-gon-cho, the songbird of sadness.
25 **Australia** The Bunyip and the Great Serpent Dragon.

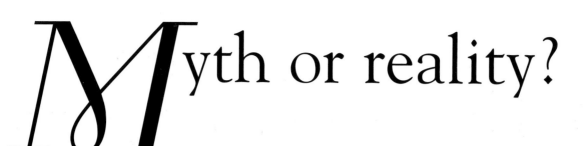

Myth or reality?

What is a dragon? A mythical creature? A fire-breathing monster? A mountain monster? A sea creature? A creature to be feared for the death and destruction it brings? The map of dragons on pages 8 and 9 shows that dragons lived all over the world, but beyond that have little in common. Sea-faring peoples feared sea monsters, like the great serpent whales of north-west Canada. Icelanders at the mercy of volcanic eruptions, dreaded the fire-breathing basilisk. The Bunyip lived in the great swamps of Australia, where brave humans might venture, but from which they rarely returned. The characters of these and all the world's other dragons suggest they are based on memories, perhaps millions of years old, of something our ancestors feared but did not understand.

No human being ever saw a dinosaur because they died out some 64 million years ago and the oldest known human remains are only about three million years old. But imagine what it must have been like to find the bones and teeth of a dinosaur. Early people had no way of knowing that the huge creatures, whose bones they had found would not loom out of the rainforests and woodlands to attack them. And if they lived where there were active volcanoes, is it any wonder they thought the monsters could breathe fire?

Man-eating, fire-breathing dragons

There were two main kinds of dragon. Some were kind, wise and benevolent, while others were fire-breathing, man-eating, creators of disaster. Dragons from the east were mostly of the first type, while western ones almost always had characteristics of the second. Dragons also symbolized the struggle between people and the natural forces of the world around them.

The dragons of disaster were feared and respected. In many legends and folktales these frightening beasts were slain by a hero, unless they killed him first. Sometimes these fearsome dragons were tamed and put to use. Greek and Roman myths tell of dragons used to guard temples and other places where treasures were kept. Not only were they fierce and strong, they also had keen eyesight.

Many dragons, especially in the Middle Ages (about 1000 to 1450), had a particular liking for young women. Heroes such as St George, whose adventures were first reported in the Middle East, bravely hunted down the dragon and rescued the maiden.

European dragons were fearsome fire-breathing monsters. They mixed elements of Greek and Roman legends (which in turn drew on myths from the Middle East, Africa and Central Asia) and monstrous wild beasts from the northern forests. With the coming of Christianity to Europe, in the 1st century AD, dragons began representing the devil.

Central American Quetzalcoatl had many forms. Here, as a plumed serpent, he devours the enemies of the Aztecs.

The 'devil' dragon

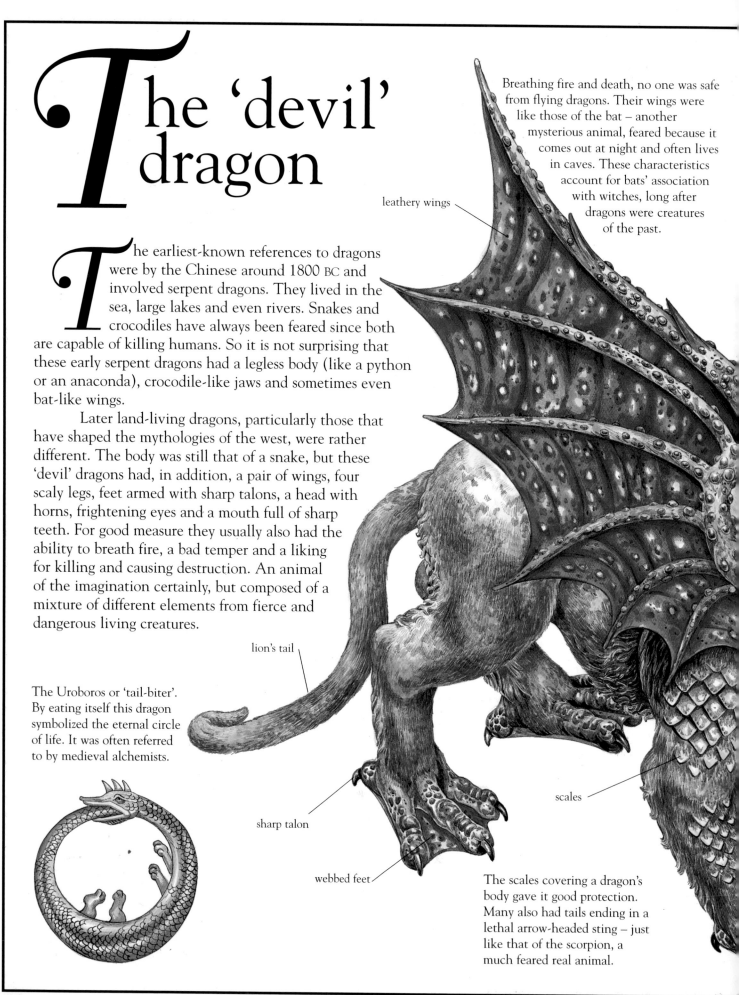

The earliest-known references to dragons were by the Chinese around 1800 BC and involved serpent dragons. They lived in the sea, large lakes and even rivers. Snakes and crocodiles have always been feared since both are capable of killing humans. So it is not surprising that these early serpent dragons had a legless body (like a python or an anaconda), crocodile-like jaws and sometimes even bat-like wings.

Later land-living dragons, particularly those that have shaped the mythologies of the west, were rather different. The body was still that of a snake, but these 'devil' dragons had, in addition, a pair of wings, four scaly legs, feet armed with sharp talons, a head with horns, frightening eyes and a mouth full of sharp teeth. For good measure they usually also had the ability to breath fire, a bad temper and a liking for killing and causing destruction. An animal of the imagination certainly, but composed of a mixture of different elements from fierce and dangerous living creatures.

Breathing fire and death, no one was safe from flying dragons. Their wings were like those of the bat – another mysterious animal, feared because it comes out at night and often lives in caves. These characteristics account for bats' association with witches, long after dragons were creatures of the past.

leathery wings

lion's tail

The Uroboros or 'tail-biter'. By eating itself this dragon symbolized the eternal circle of life. It was often referred to by medieval alchemists.

sharp talon

webbed feet

scales

The scales covering a dragon's body gave it good protection. Many also had tails ending in a lethal arrow-headed sting – just like that of the scorpion, a much feared real animal.

In medieval times the devil was believed to take the form of a dragon. Disguised like this, he would enter homes, wrecking them, and terrifying or even killing those inside.

wattle

bird-like wings

scaly, snake-like body

legless body

The amphitere (above), which often features in legends from Egypt and the Middle East, was a fearsome beast that terrified travellers. It had the body of a snake, the head of a dragon, the wings of a bird and the wattle of a cockerel (also known as a rooster).

A scaly, horned winged dragon attacks and kills a lion, based on a scene embroidered on a 16th-century tapestry. Both monster and lion are of a similar size, which suggests the dragon was actually a dragonet. Dragonets were small dragons, but their size was no measure of their power as they were often more deadly than their larger cousins.

horns

In the Middle Ages a dragonet caused havoc around Mount Pilatus, near Wilser in Switzerland. The only person prepared to face it was a convicted murderer, who was promised his freedom if he killed it. He did, but a drop of the dragonet's blood splashed his hand and killed him.

Dragon slayers

Male and female, light and darkness, good and evil: the dragon was used to represent the coming together of the opposite forces which occur in all of us (see below). This was particularly true of early Christian and Muslim cultures.

Dragon-slaying legends occur in cultures wherever the monsters were vicious. In these tales good (the slayer) overcomes evil (the dragon). Both the Christian and Islamic worlds used dragons to illustrate the dangers of evil.

In Christian stories, the archangel Michael was skilled at killing dragons. However, of all the dragon slayers, St George, the patron saint of Barcelona and England, is the best known.

St George, a knight in shining armour, was born in Lydda, near Jerusalem (although the English later claimed Coventry as his birthplace) and had been a soldier in the Roman army before converting to Christianity. Travelling around Europe and the Middle East on his horse, St George slew many dragons. Since dragons were forms of the Devil himself, it was quite natural for George, a Christian, to take them on and rid the world of evil.

In Europe the lance was believed to be the best weapon for killing a dragon. But it had to be thrust deep into the monster's mouth to ensure a kill, because scaly armour protected the rest of the dragon's body.

Long ago the Illini tribe of Illinois were troubled by a dragon bird, the Piasa (below left), which developed a taste for human flesh. Masatonga, a young warrior, proposed a way of killing the dreadful beast. He offered to act as bait, to lure the dragon into the woods. Once among the trees, the dragon was forced to fold its wings, becoming vulnerable to the poisoned arrows fired by hidden warriors there.

There are different stories about how St George met his death. In some he was roasted, in others crushed, beheaded or buried alive. But perhaps the dragons won in the end, for one version claims he was poisoned by dragon's blood!

Heroes of ancient Persia also had to prove their courage by confronting and slaying a dragon. Their dragons looked more like those found in China than Europe, which probably reflects the ancient trade links between Persia and the Far East.

In Mesopotamian mythology the defeat of Tiamat, one of the first two beings, by the god Marduk resulted in the creation of man. Marduk then became the supreme god and under his protection the great city of Babylon was built on the River Euphrates (now in Iraq).

*F*rightening dragons

Tales of dragons depended on the skill of the storyteller and listeners' imaginations for their fearsomeness. Depicting them, however, was another matter. As three-dimensional objects dragons could become even more savage and terrifying, taking on the size and appearance of real monsters. In doing so they could be used to terrify enemies as an army went into battle. Emblazoned on banners and shields, these dragons represented the power and strength of those who used the symbol.

Among the best-known warriors using the dragon symbol were the Vikings. The dragon-headed longships of these dreaded marauders caused fear and panic wherever they were sighted. This was certainly true among the Christian communities of north-western Europe between AD 800 and 1000. It confirmed their belief that the dragon symbolized all the forces of evil in the world.

At only four days' old, the Greek god Apollo, son of Zeus, used a bow and arrow to slay the dragon Python at Delphi in Greece (above). This proved he was a worthy son of his father, the greatest of the Greeks' gods.

Jupiter (the Roman name for the god Zeus) used a thunderbolt to overcome the dragon Typhon (below). Then he imprisoned it beneath Mount Etna, a very active volcano on the Mediterranean island of Sicily, south of Italy.

A Greek epic tells of the voyage of Jason and the Argonauts and their quest for the Golden Fleece which was guarded by a fierce dragon. This scene, painted on an Etruscan vase, shows Jason being spat out alive by the dragon because of the intervention of the goddess Athena.

Jason

Athena

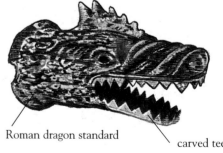

Roman dragon standard

carved teeth

The Roman cavalry carried special standards which had the heads of dragons (above) and tails of coloured cloth which hissed like snakes as they blew in the wind. The noise helped to unsettle enemies and gave the impression that the attacking force was larger than it really was.

The Vikings deliberately made their longships appear even more frightening to their enemies by carving a magnificent dragon's head at the top of each ship's bow.

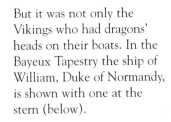

But it was not only the Vikings who had dragons' heads on their boats. In the Bayeux Tapestry the ship of William, Duke of Normandy, is shown with one at the stern (below).

According to the Old Testament book of Daniel, dragons could be killed with a concoction of fat, hair and pitch. This, of course, meant dragon slayers had to get very close to their prey. A 14th century stained glass panel (left) in the church of St Etienne, Mulhouse, France, shows Daniel giving a dragon the fatal mixture.

Nordic mythology tells of many strange and fierce monsters. On an ancient Scandinavian door (right) the dragon Fafnir is shown in violent battle with the hero Sigurd. After killing the dragon, Sigurd roasted its heart over a fire, tasted its blood and was instantly able to understand the language of the birds.

In medieval times the dragon was adopted as a heraldic decoration. Anyone entitled to a coat of arms could use a dragon as part of their arms, as long as it was approved by the Royal College of Heralds (who still carry out this role). Oliver Cromwell (1599-1658) used a dragon on his coat of arms (left). Shown rampant (with fore-legs raised), wings endorsed (held above the back), and with a nowed (knotted) tail, the dragon represents strength, invincibility and fierceness.

lion

dragon

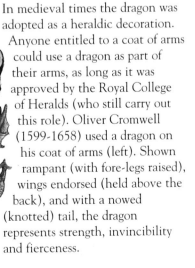

PAX·QVÆRITVR·BELLO

The coat of arms of Gray's Inn, one of the four Inns of Court in London to which lawyers must belong, depicts a dragon (below). This is to encourage fear and respect of the law.

Heracles & the Hydra

Classical Greek mythology has many stories of heroes overcoming monsters. One of the best-known is how Heracles killed the many-headed Hydra. In payment for crimes he had committed, Heracles (more commonly known by his Roman name, Hercules) was given 12, very difficult, if not impossible, tasks by the King of Mycenae. These were named the Labours of Heracles. The second of these was to find and kill the dreaded Hydra.

The creature lived in a cave near Lerna in the Lernean Swamp. The monster was killing people and devastating the countryside. Everything about the creature was deadly, even the scent of its tracks. The goddess Athena guided Heracles to the Hydra's lair where he flung flaming torches into the cave, forcing the Hydra into the open. When the monster's heads saw Heracles they hissed with rage and lunged at him. Heracles swung his club to smash the heads. But as one was destroyed, two more replaced it. Undaunted, Heracles swung his club again, but this time also plunged a burning torch into the smashed mass of the monster. This stopped new heads growing. Eventually only one head remained, and this Heracles sliced off with his sword.

Friendly dragons

Of all the dragons in the world, the Chinese ones were the most revered. Unlike many western dragons, those of the Orient were harmless, good, kind, intelligent and friendly. Some were even regarded as domestic animals! These Oriental dragons were closely linked to the two main Chinese religions: Buddhism and Taoism. Only rarely did Chinese dragons come into conflict with gods, heroes and people, in sharp contrast to their fearsome European cousins. As a result there are no myths of dragon-slaying in the east.

The Oriental dragons were descendants of the Indian nagas, which were quite aggressive, although not as fierce as European dragons. It is through these Indian relatives that Chinese dragons were linked with the earth and sky by means of water. They brought clouds and rain and dictated the seasons, in this way influencing the lives of people. They also lived under water where they were safe, particularly from the enemy they feared most: the many-legged centipede.

The Chinese believe in many different types of dragon, and almost every aspect of daily life has its own special guardian dragon. The years in the Chinese calendar are named after different animals and one of these is the dragon. Dragons are highly regarded because they are an essential part of Chinese beliefs and culture and this is depicted in statues, bronzes, on doorways, on printed silk, embroidered on ceremonial robes and painted or printed on ceramics. They even appear in mahjong, a game of chance.

Both Chinese and Indian myths describe dragons that changed shape whenever they liked. Vritra, the demonic Indian dragon, is often shown as a cloud-like-serpent writhing around mountain tops. This link with mountains and clouds may explain why many eastern dragons were associated with the weather, especially rain. The thunder and lightning which so often accompany storms, particularly around mountains, were seen as signs that the dragon was awake and on the move.

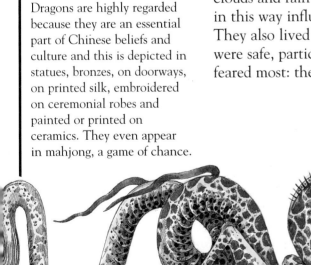

According to ancient Chinese mythology a dragon was made up of nine parts. The number nine is very important in Chinese beliefs as it represents *yang*, one of the two interlocking parts of the universe. After hatching from its egg, a dragon took 4000 years to change into its final winged form.

Dragon fire was the opposite of earthly fire: if it touched water it burnt more fiercely. Dragons were afraid of centipedes, coloured thread and certain plants.

Dragons' eyes were hurt by the 'taste' of gold and iron.

The lump on a dragon's head enabled it to fly.

antlers of a stag

ears of a cow

eyes of a demon

Dragons' breath turned to clouds, rain and lightning.

The scales beneath a dragon's chin faced the wrong way. Humans died if they touched them.

face of a camel

20

scales of a fish

belly of a clam

Dragons' favourite meal was roast swallows so when people wanted rain, they offered these to them.

tiger's feet for speed and stealth

talons of an eagle

body of a snake

Nine parts of a dragon

The dragon was the origin of all creatures, winged, hairy, scaly and armoured. So, according to Way Fu of the Han Dynasty (206BC – AD220) dragons are made up of nine parts, each, except for the eyes, representing a different animal. Each dragon had 117 scales covering its body. Of these, 81 contained goodness and 36 evil, so a Chinese dragon was more good than bad! This double-sided nature showed up in its voice which was neither very pleasant nor very frightening. Male dragons owed their supernatural power and great strength to a large luminous 'pearl of knowledge' hidden among the skin folds beneath their chin.

The songbird of sadness

Ti lung, the Oriental dragon of rivers, sea and land, lived in the sea in springtime, but in autumn ascended to the heavens.

Oriental sages could tell the difference between male and female dragons. Males had horns that were concave, steep and wavy, thick at the top and thin below. Females, on the other hand, had a round mane, thin scales, a strong tail and a straight nose.

Female dragons laid beautiful gem-like eggs. Any brightly coloured stone was believed to be a dragon's egg.

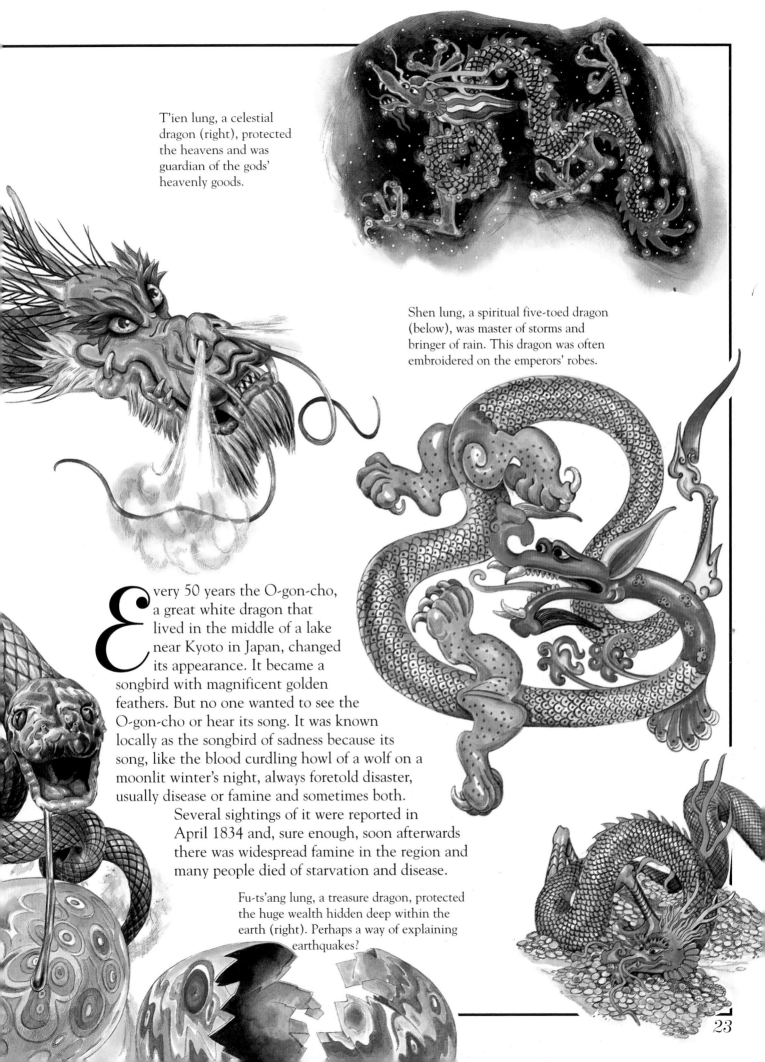

T'ien lung, a celestial dragon (right), protected the heavens and was guardian of the gods' heavenly goods.

Shen lung, a spiritual five-toed dragon (below), was master of storms and bringer of rain. This dragon was often embroidered on the emperors' robes.

Every 50 years the O-gon-cho, a great white dragon that lived in the middle of a lake near Kyoto in Japan, changed its appearance. It became a songbird with magnificent golden feathers. But no one wanted to see the O-gon-cho or hear its song. It was known locally as the songbird of sadness because its song, like the blood curdling howl of a wolf on a moonlit winter's night, always foretold disaster, usually disease or famine and sometimes both.

Several sightings of it were reported in April 1834 and, sure enough, soon afterwards there was widespread famine in the region and many people died of starvation and disease.

Fu-ts'ang lung, a treasure dragon, protected the huge wealth hidden deep within the earth (right). Perhaps a way of explaining earthquakes?

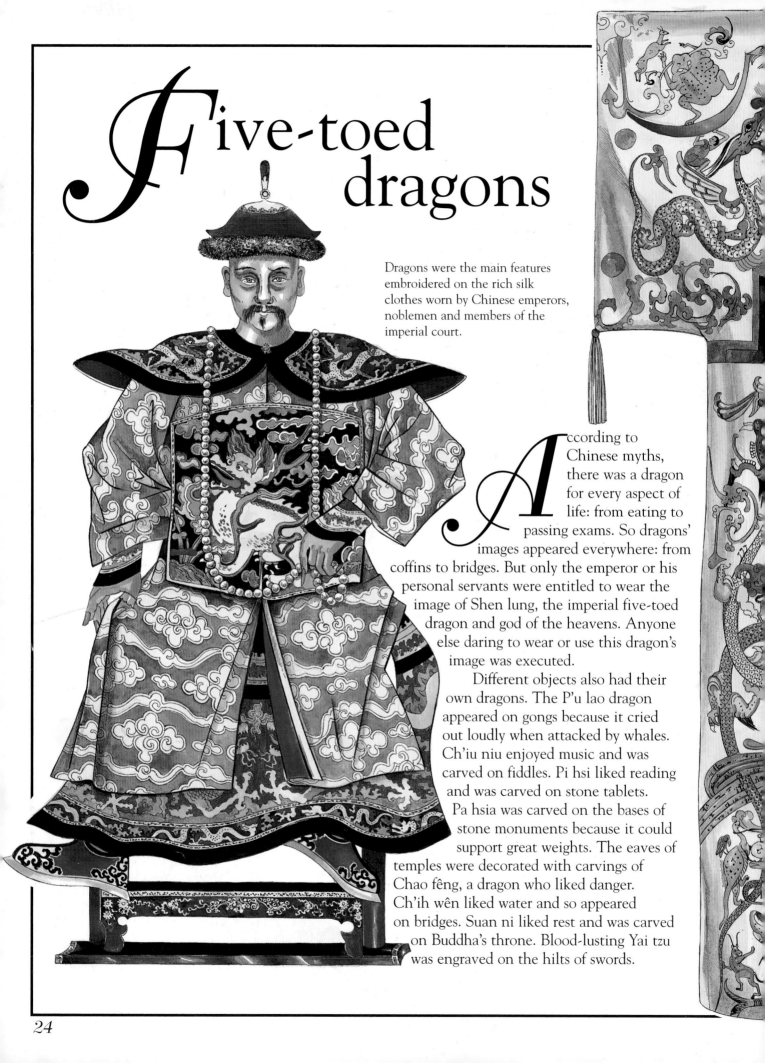

Five-toed dragons

Dragons were the main features embroidered on the rich silk clothes worn by Chinese emperors, noblemen and members of the imperial court.

According to Chinese myths, there was a dragon for every aspect of life: from eating to passing exams. So dragons' images appeared everywhere: from coffins to bridges. But only the emperor or his personal servants were entitled to wear the image of Shen lung, the imperial five-toed dragon and god of the heavens. Anyone else daring to wear or use this dragon's image was executed.

Different objects also had their own dragons. The P'u lao dragon appeared on gongs because it cried out loudly when attacked by whales. Ch'iu niu enjoyed music and was carved on fiddles. Pi hsi liked reading and was carved on stone tablets. Pa hsia was carved on the bases of stone monuments because it could support great weights. The eaves of temples were decorated with carvings of Chao fêng, a dragon who liked danger. Ch'ih wên liked water and so appeared on bridges. Suan ni liked rest and was carved on Buddha's throne. Blood-lusting Yai tzu was engraved on the hilts of swords.

The ceramics made by craftsmen in China during the Ming period (mid 14th to early 17th centuries) were particularly fine. Dragons were popular decorations on vases and plates.

Japanese prints and drawings often depict dragons. In this print by Kunisadam, the old wise-woman Tai-shin and two attendants fly across the ocean on the back of a white dragon.

Tai-shin

Japanese dragons were similar to those found in China. The main differences were that Japanese dragons had a more snake-like body, only three claws on each foot and they did not fly as much.

bushy eyebrows

nostrils

When a Chinese noblewoman, the Lady Dai, died 2200 years ago she was buried in a tomb with a silk banner showing the universe. Below her was the underworld full of monsters. Above her were the heavens with the sun and the moon, and large dragons flying beyond the heavenly gates.

The tatsu was the most common of the Japanese dragons. They were associated with the sea.

three-clawed foot

snake-like body

The story of Dragon-mother

Long, long ago, when the world was much younger, an old lady was walking beside a river. There before her, lying in the grass on the river's bank, she saw five beautiful stones. Gently she picked them up. They were so beautiful that she carried them away to her home, where she looked at them and marvelled at their beauty many times a day.

Time passed, then one day there was the most terrible storm. Amid thunder, rain and darkness, the five stones hatched, for they were in fact dragon's eggs. The old woman gathered up the baby dragons, which looked like tiny snakes, and stumbling through the pouring rain made her way back to the river bank. There, very gently, she let the little creatures wriggle free into the water.

The dragons that lived in the river were so pleased that she had returned their children that they gave her a special gift – the power of foretelling the future. When the old woman was washing clothes in the river, the fish, which are the servants of the dragons, used to dance before her. Everyone knew her and what she had done and that she was a wise-woman. She was known throughout the land as 'Dragon-mother'.

The old lady became so famous that the Emperor commanded her to come to court so he could ask her for advice. So she set out to obey the Emperor's command to visit his court. But she was old and the journey was long and she died on her way. Because she was famous she was given a fine funeral and buried on the river's eastern bank. This, however, was the wrong side of the river and the dragons were very angry. They did not like their old friend being treated badly and they whipped up a violent storm. Next day, when the storm had died down and the weather was calm once more, everyone saw that Dragon-mother's grave was on the opposite side of the river, though no one could be certain how this had happened.

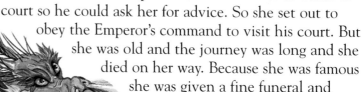

Mysterious dragons

Strange, mysterious dragons roamed the world. To many people they were all-powerful, god-like creatures to be worshipped, feared and respected. Even if they were not gods themselves, they were servants of the gods.

As befits their mysterious nature, their birth was also a matter of strangeness and wonder. Eastern dragons metamorphosed, changing as a caterpillar changes into a butterfly. But it was a long process – 4000 years.

Dragons laid their eggs near water, for even though many lived on land, their ancestors were water creatures. After 1000 years a water snake hatched from the egg. After 500 years this grew the head of a carp and was known as kiao. Another 1000 years passed and it had a fish-like body, covered in scales, but with four short legs with four sharp claws on each foot, an elongated tail and a bearded face. It was then a kiao-lung ('lung' means 'deaf'). In the next 500 years the dragon grew horns, through which it could hear. At this stage it was known as a kioh-lung. The long metamorphosis continued. After another 1000 years had passed, the dragon grew delicate wings. This was a ying-lung or winged dragon. And, at last, the dragon's metamorphosis was complete.

Many dragons feared humans as much as humans feared dragons. Such dragons hid away, avoiding humans altogether. The Haida people of the American north-west tell of one such serpent dragon. A solitary creature, it lived on its own. But when the winter storms came and people kept inside, they knew it was on the prowl.

Dragons in religion

Human imagination has produced many weird and mysterious forms of dragon. Those that had snake-like bodies, horns and crocodile-like jaws were the most common. Some had legs, but relatively few had wings.

This giant man-eating monster (above) appeared throughout Aztec art. It was often shown carved on altars.

To protect the dead, the ancient Egyptians often painted Mertseger (below), a flying dragon, part bird, part snake, in tombs in the Valley of the Queens. This image is similar to those of Osiris, the imperial dragon and lord of the dead.

At the centre of Indian creation was Ananta, a giant many-headed monster and ruler of all other snakes. This painting (right) shows the god Krishna climbing on its many heads.

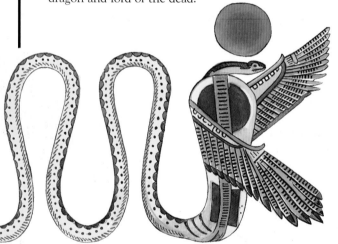

Indian dragons mix elements of Middle Eastern and Chinese dragons.

In ancient Rome priestesses known as vestal virgins looked after fearsome serpents (right). A priestess's purity was assessed by the way the serpents reacted to her.

Buddha sits on the coiled body of a naga, a dragon monster-god of India (right). The naga's hooded head which shields Buddha shows clearly that this monster was based on the cobra.

Many dragons were said to live in or near water. This is not really surprising, for water is essential for everyone, everywhere: without water life is not possible. Equally it is not surprising that the commonest dragons combined elements of snakes and crocodiles, for both live in or near water. They are also dangerous to humans. So it is a short step to believing they control the water that humans need. For the same reason many dragons were associated with fertility.

Without water, crops cannot grow. Therefore, if dragons control water in rivers, why not rain too? Thus, whether it was the annual flood of the River Nile in ancient Egypt or the monsoons of the Indian sub-continent that brought growth and fertility to the fields, dragons were believed to play a part.

To defeat a rival, Medshelemet, a shaman or witch doctor, turned into Wewilmekq, a 12 metre long serpent-dragon (right). The trick worked, with Wewilmekq beating his rival decisively.

In Australia, the Aborigines believe in Dreamtime, a period before Creation. At this time Earth was a desolate place and many supernatural beings slept. The Great Serpent Dragon (below) caused a flood to wash away this early world and it was replaced by the world of today.

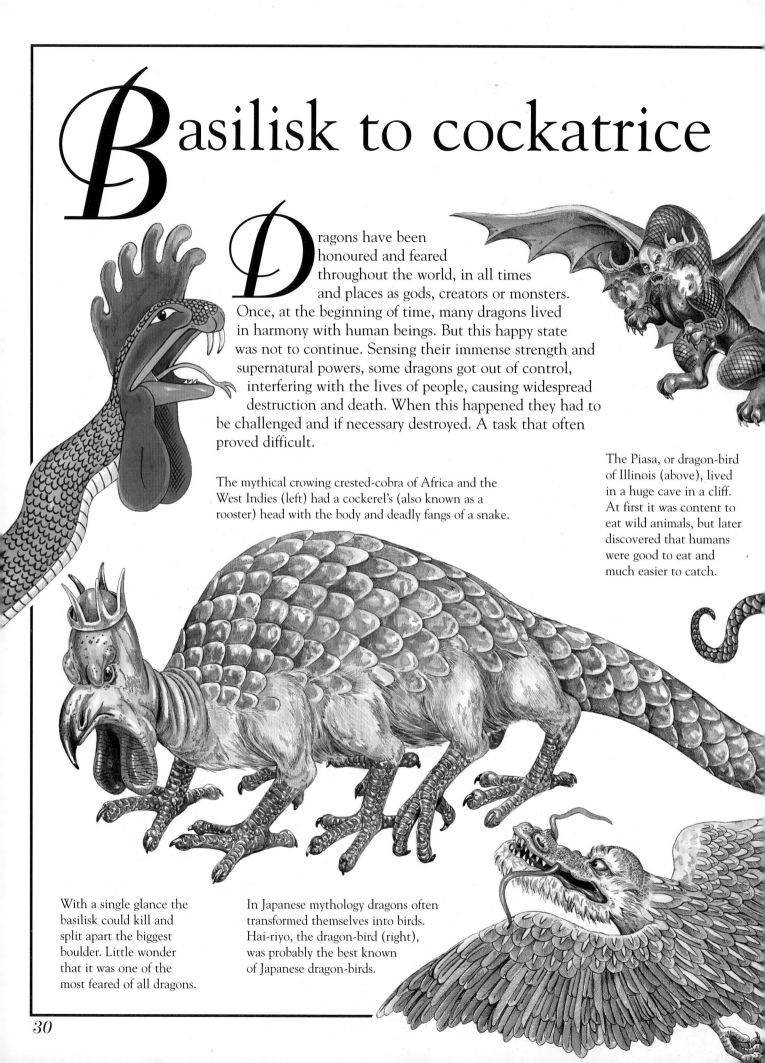

Basilisk to cockatrice

Dragons have been honoured and feared throughout the world, in all times and places as gods, creators or monsters. Once, at the beginning of time, many dragons lived in harmony with human beings. But this happy state was not to continue. Sensing their immense strength and supernatural powers, some dragons got out of control, interfering with the lives of people, causing widespread destruction and death. When this happened they had to be challenged and if necessary destroyed. A task that often proved difficult.

The mythical crowing crested-cobra of Africa and the West Indies (left) had a cockerel's (also known as a rooster) head with the body and deadly fangs of a snake.

The Piasa, or dragon-bird of Illinois (above), lived in a huge cave in a cliff. At first it was content to eat wild animals, but later discovered that humans were good to eat and much easier to catch.

With a single glance the basilisk could kill and split apart the biggest boulder. Little wonder that it was one of the most feared of all dragons.

In Japanese mythology dragons often transformed themselves into birds. Hai-riyo, the dragon-bird (right), was probably the best known of Japanese dragon-birds.

The only way to kill a cockatrice, which was like the basilisk, was to face it with a mirror. When it saw itself it would die of shock.

Unlike most other snake-like dragons which slithered across the ground, the basilisk held its body upright.

The basilisk underwent its final transformation to become a cockatrice in medieval times. Its legs and head became bird-like, it grew wings and developed a spiked tail. Its character, however, did not change. It remained as dangerous as it had always been.

In Australia, long ago, a boy caught a baby Bunyip. Furious, its mother flooded the land. When the baby Bunyip was set free the floods went down and the boy and his friends swam away – as black swans.

Serpent dragons and dragon whales abound in the folktales of countries bordering a sea or ocean. The huge monster (above) that inhabited the waters off the north-west coast of Canada is typical of these creatures.

The French river monster Peluda (left), breathed fire and spat venom. With a body protected by poisonous quills, the monster was safe. However, the fiancé of one of its intended victims cut off its tail, its only weak spot, and killed it.

In Hindu mythology Varuna, the water god, and his steed Makara, a water monster, represented water's divine power.

Serpents

There are hundreds of legends of sea serpents and sea dragons from around the world. As they were told and retold, these stories brought back by returning explorers inevitably became exaggerated and distorted. Leviathan, the largest and most terrifying serpent of them all, is described in the Bible in the Old Testament book of Isaiah. It could drink rivers dry and eat dragons 1600km long as if they were mice.

But are these tales really so extraordinary? The early sailors were voyaging into completely unknown waters. In tiny boats, peering through rain and fog, it is not surprising that a group of whales, basking at the surface, seemed even larger than they really were. How do you describe a half-glimpsed hammerhead shark to someone who has never seen one? Once ashore, even the most sober sailor might begin to doubt what he had seen. In the midst of a storm, could you really be sure those terrible things flailing at you were the 10-metre tentacles of a giant squid and not Scylla's awful heads?

Many of the world's deepest lakes are inhabited by legendary monsters. One of these is said to live in Loch Ness in Scotland (below). The Loch Ness Monster has been tantalizing people for years. All sorts of sophisticated equipment has been used to locate it, without success. But sightings of Nessie, as the creature is affectionately called, are still regularly reported.

On his long voyage home after the siege of Troy, the Greek hero Odysseus had to sail past the monster Scylla (left), with its six heads on long, writhing necks. If he tried to avoid it, his ship would be sucked into the whirlpool Charybdis.

Tiamat and Marduk

In the beginning, according to ancient Babylonian belief, there were two beings, Apsu and Tiamat. Apsu the male represented space and fresh water, while Tiamat the female represented chaos and the sea. These two beings were the parents of many gods. After a while the gods became quarrelsome, as siblings do. Apsu became tired of this, but Tiamat defended her offspring. Losing patience, Apsu plotted to kill the gods. His plotting was overheard by them and he was killed by Ea, who took over Apsu's palace. Ea and his wife then had a son called Marduk.

Tiamat was furious. She created a huge army of monsters to avenge Apsu's death and transformed herself into a dragon. Her body was like a serpent's, covered in impenetrable scales. She had a long neck held upright, curved horns on her head and feet armed with savage talons. Horrified, the other gods did not know what to do. Several heroes tried to overcome Tiamat and her forces but failed. Finally, Marduk agreed to fight her. With the aid of a net he caught her and flung a hurricane in her face. As she opened her monstrous mouth to devour Marduk the hurricane swept in. It gripped her heart in fingers of ice and inflated her body. Just at the right moment Marduk shot an arrow into her stomach, unprotected by scales, killing her. Immediately he sliced Tiamat apart, splitting her into two and carving her up until she was unrecognizable. Due to his success, Marduk became the supreme god.

Marduk had no trouble dealing with Tiamat's followers once they realized she was dead. He killed them all in order to rebuild the world himself. Half of Tiamat's body became the heavens which he scattered with stars. The other half, the earth, he covered in forests, fields, rivers, mountains and wild life. To people the earth, he created humans from the blood spurting out of the body of Kingu, one of Tiamat's supporters.

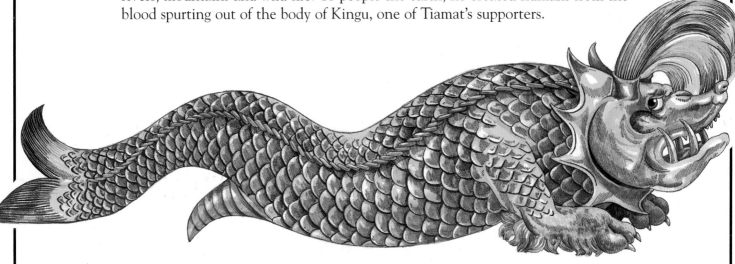

Living dragons?

In the distant past gigantic creatures roamed the earth: dinosaurs on land, pterosaurs in the air and pliosaurs and plesiosaurs in the seas. Today, of course, they are all extinct. But, even now, living in the seas, rivers and on land there are many fierce and strange animals: huge snakes, lizards and crocodiles. These living dragons have much in common: their size, sharp teeth and, frequently, a scaly body. Most of them live in tropical and subtropical parts of the world where they are often shy of humans, hiding away and rarely being seen. In addition they are all carnivorous, feeding on live animals and dead carcasses.

When dragon stories were commonplace early travellers seeing these living monsters at a distance for the first time, could easily think they were dragons. The huge monitor lizards of Africa, south-east Asia and Australia are perfect models on which to base a dragon. Add bat-like wings and the ability to breath fire and you have a typical dragon. And it has been suggested that the source of the story about the dragonet of Mount Pilatus lies in the fossilized skeletons of pterodactyls, prehistoric flying reptiles, that have been found nearby.

Alligators, crocodiles and their relative, the Indian gharial, are among the largest of living reptiles. They have long scaly bodies and tails, clawed feet, staring eyes and vicious teeth. These characteristics, together with their watery habitats, make them the likely source of many dragon myths. And, like their mythical counterparts, they may even eat human flesh.

Fishy fakes

The great age of exploration that began in the 15th century gave dragons a new lease of life. Many of the travellers and voyagers returned with amazing tales of incredible creatures glimpsed through rainforest, heat haze or sea fog. How do you describe a camel so that people will believe you? Or a gila monster? Or a dugong? Illustrated books of travellers' tales became very popular.

It was not long before unscrupulous people began making models of these 'real' creatures, and indeed creating entirely new ones, from parts of different species of common birds and animals. There was a ready market for these fakes among gullible people interested in natural history. This creative forgery received a boost in the 18th century when educated people from northern Europe started travelling to the Mediterranean and wanted souvenirs of their travels. But this was not just a European phenomenon. In 1784 a man-faced cockatrice was reported to emerge regularly from Lake Fagua in Chile. It, too, proved to be a hoax.

Many fake dragons (above) were made from parts of fish. Skates and rays, with their spiny skins and tails, were a common source of body parts for fake dragons. When alive, these flat fish (below) live and feed on the seabed, but are frequently caught in fishermen's nets or washed ashore by storms.

tail of a skate or ray

wing of a skate becomes a dragon's wing

coils of a python or other large snake

patterned scales

Snakes have long scaly bodies. Most hiss and many are poisonous. It is amazing how many newly hatched dragons looked just like snakes!

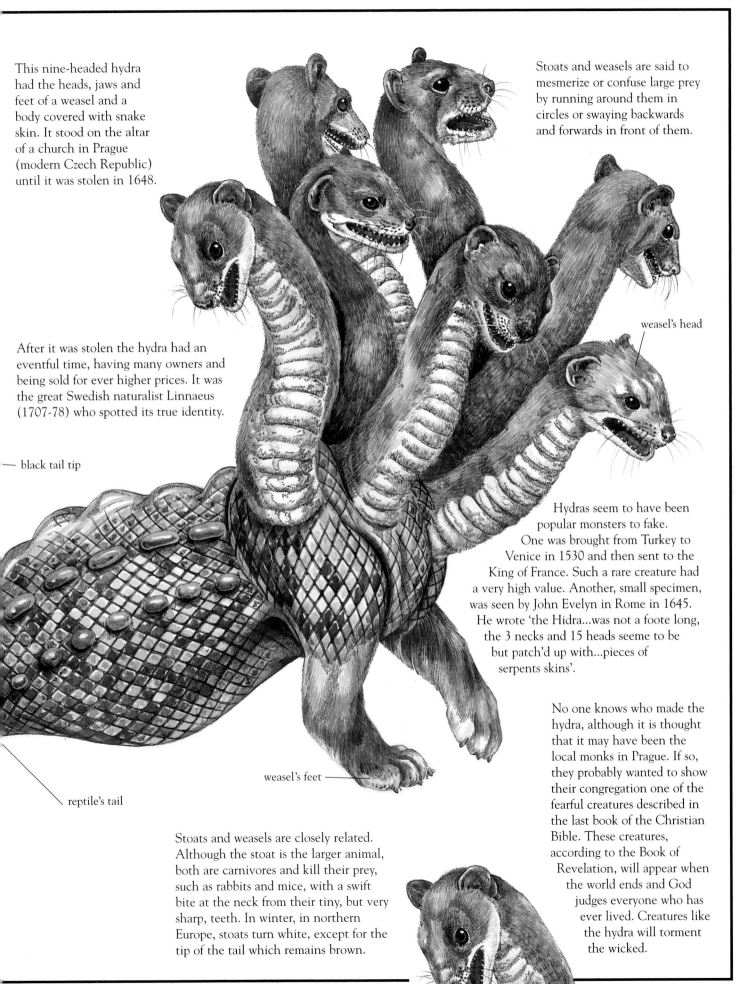

This nine-headed hydra had the heads, jaws and feet of a weasel and a body covered with snake skin. It stood on the altar of a church in Prague (modern Czech Republic) until it was stolen in 1648.

Stoats and weasels are said to mesmerize or confuse large prey by running around them in circles or swaying backwards and forwards in front of them.

After it was stolen the hydra had an eventful time, having many owners and being sold for ever higher prices. It was the great Swedish naturalist Linnaeus (1707-78) who spotted its true identity.

— black tail tip

weasel's head

Hydras seem to have been popular monsters to fake. One was brought from Turkey to Venice in 1530 and then sent to the King of France. Such a rare creature had a very high value. Another, small specimen, was seen by John Evelyn in Rome in 1645. He wrote 'the Hidra...was not a foote long, the 3 necks and 15 heads seeme to be but patch'd up with...pieces of serpents skins'.

No one knows who made the hydra, although it is thought that it may have been the local monks in Prague. If so, they probably wanted to show their congregation one of the fearful creatures described in the last book of the Christian Bible. These creatures, according to the Book of Revelation, will appear when the world ends and God judges everyone who has ever lived. Creatures like the hydra will torment the wicked.

reptile's tail

weasel's feet

Stoats and weasels are closely related. Although the stoat is the larger animal, both are carnivores and kill their prey, such as rabbits and mice, with a swift bite at the neck from their tiny, but very sharp, teeth. In winter, in northern Europe, stoats turn white, except for the tip of the tail which remains brown.

The real thing?

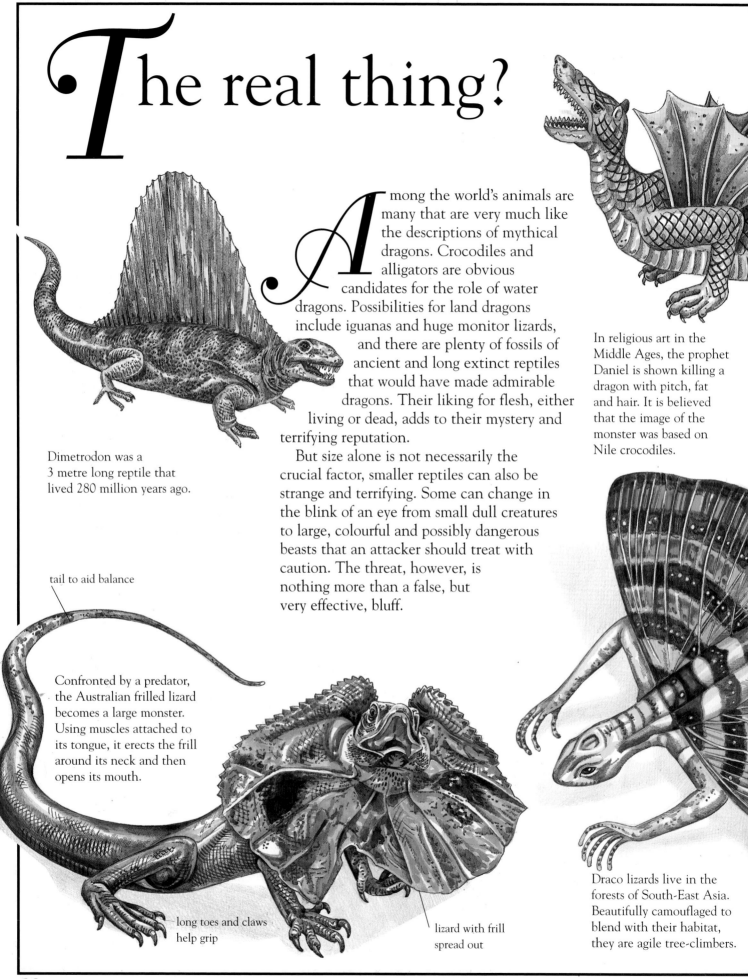

Among the world's animals are many that are very much like the descriptions of mythical dragons. Crocodiles and alligators are obvious candidates for the role of water dragons. Possibilities for land dragons include iguanas and huge monitor lizards, and there are plenty of fossils of ancient and long extinct reptiles that would have made admirable dragons. Their liking for flesh, either living or dead, adds to their mystery and terrifying reputation.

But size alone is not necessarily the crucial factor, smaller reptiles can also be strange and terrifying. Some can change in the blink of an eye from small dull creatures to large, colourful and possibly dangerous beasts that an attacker should treat with caution. The threat, however, is nothing more than a false, but very effective, bluff.

Dimetrodon was a 3 metre long reptile that lived 280 million years ago.

In religious art in the Middle Ages, the prophet Daniel is shown killing a dragon with pitch, fat and hair. It is believed that the image of the monster was based on Nile crocodiles.

tail to aid balance

Confronted by a predator, the Australian frilled lizard becomes a large monster. Using muscles attached to its tongue, it erects the frill around its neck and then opens its mouth.

long toes and claws help grip

lizard with frill spread out

Draco lizards live in the forests of South-East Asia. Beautifully camouflaged to blend with their habitat, they are agile tree-climbers.

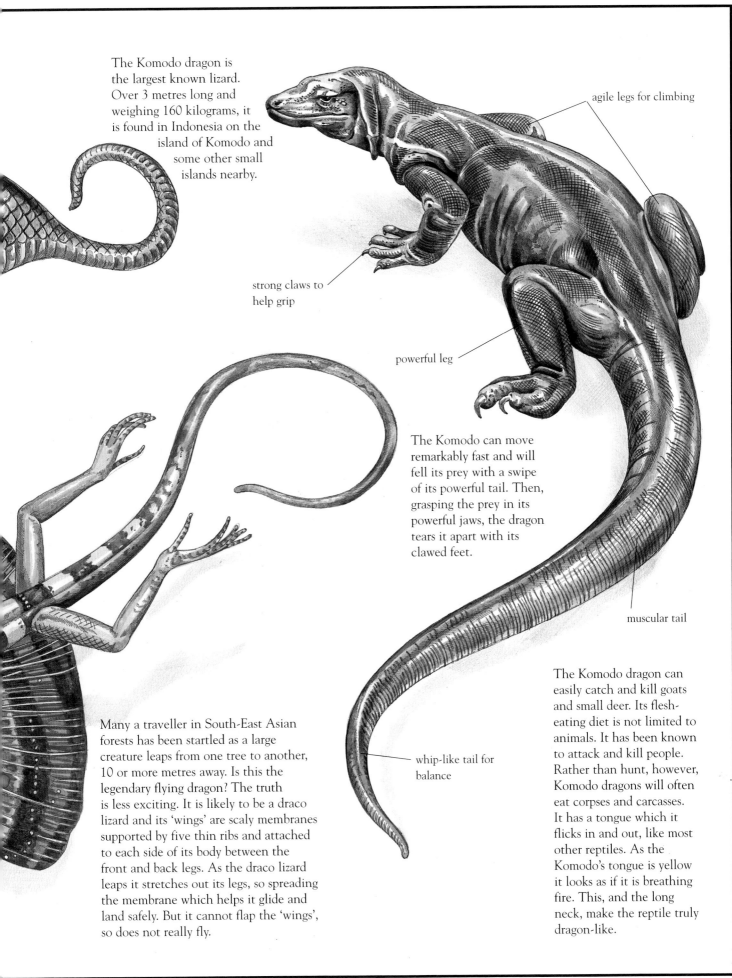

The Komodo dragon is the largest known lizard. Over 3 metres long and weighing 160 kilograms, it is found in Indonesia on the island of Komodo and some other small islands nearby.

agile legs for climbing

strong claws to help grip

powerful leg

The Komodo can move remarkably fast and will fell its prey with a swipe of its powerful tail. Then, grasping the prey in its powerful jaws, the dragon tears it apart with its clawed feet.

muscular tail

whip-like tail for balance

Many a traveller in South-East Asian forests has been startled as a large creature leaps from one tree to another, 10 or more metres away. Is this the legendary flying dragon? The truth is less exciting. It is likely to be a draco lizard and its 'wings' are scaly membranes supported by five thin ribs and attached to each side of its body between the front and back legs. As the draco lizard leaps it stretches out its legs, so spreading the membrane which helps it glide and land safely. But it cannot flap the 'wings', so does not really fly.

The Komodo dragon can easily catch and kill goats and small deer. Its flesh-eating diet is not limited to animals. It has been known to attack and kill people. Rather than hunt, however, Komodo dragons will often eat corpses and carcasses. It has a tongue which it flicks in and out, like most other reptiles. As the Komodo's tongue is yellow it looks as if it is breathing fire. This, and the long neck, make the reptile truly dragon-like.

Fantastic fantasies

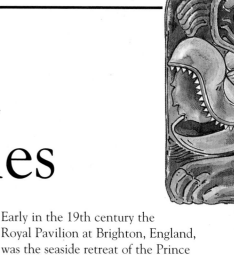

The dragon is the luckiest Chinese birth sign. Dragon people are energetic, strong-willed and protective. But they are also ambitious and unreliable and may be bad tempered.

Dragons have been brought to life in many forms. They have been drawn, painted, printed, embroidered, tiled, carved, moulded and cast. Though these monstrous creatures have meant different things to different peoples, common to all beliefs are the dragon's power, strength and fearsome nature.

Symbolizing this power and strength, dragons were woven or embroidered on Chinese imperial robes and carved on Vikings' longships. All over the world they appear on buildings, but they are especially common in the Far East. Here buildings are decorated with dragon roof ornaments, tiles, building stones, gates, steps and balustrades. Bridges bear dragon shapes in honour of the river dragons. In Europe, dragons are used on and in old Christian churches to ward off evil spirits and to represent the devil and evil. They are also depicted on tombs and altars. But they also have a lighter side, being used to decorate furniture, china and other ornaments. And there is, of course, the splendid creature that is the centrepiece of every Chinese dragon dance!

Early in the 19th century the Royal Pavilion at Brighton, England, was the seaside retreat of the Prince Regent. It is full of oriental designs. This metre-long carved, painted and silvered dragon originally had a chandelier hanging from it.

Sirrush, a Babylonian dragon decorates the gate to Ishtar's temple, Babylon. It is likely that its long, upright neck reflects travellers' tales of giraffes.

A tombstone in the churchyard of St Paul's Cathedral, London, shows a stag fighting a dragon. The scene was probably carved by a Norse artist early in the 11th century.

Gargoyles, the spouts draining rain from the roofs of old buildings, get their name from the French 'gargouille' after the terrible water-spouting monster that threatened Rouen, northern France, in 1520.

Dragon-like gods appear on
Central American Mayan altars
(above). They often have two
heads, but we do not know
what they represent.

Carved dragons appear
throughout Thailand.
This one (above) forms
the balustrade beside the
steps leading to a temple.

In the myth of the Hesperides
a winged dragon guarded the garden
at the end of the world where beautiful nymphs
lived. Antoni Gaudi copied this idea for his
gates (above) to the Güell Pavilions
in Barcelona, Spain.

Gaudi also designed
the wrought iron
dragons that guard
the steps of the Parc
Güell in Barcelona.

Dragon 'facts'

The word 'dragon' comes from the Greek 'drakon' for a very large snake. The Romans used the word 'draco'.

In ancient China travellers who had just eaten roast swallows were advised not to cross rivers or lakes, because the dragons living there would smell their favourite food and attack the traveller.

The town of Tarascon in France gets its name from the tarasque, a dreadful river monster that lived nearby and devastated the region in the Middle Ages. The town's original name was Nerluc.

Several ancient religions had dragons at the centre of their beliefs. Dragons created the earth and human beings as well as controlling the wind, rain, rivers and seas.

The male quetzal of Central America had four tail feathers over 60 centimetres long. As it flew they undulated and looked just like a flying snake – one of the forms of the Aztecs' god Quetzalcoatl.

Greek and Roman myths are full of stories of dragon-like monsters. These are typically found, fought and killed by heroes like Odysseus, Heracles, Jason and Perseus.

The tatzelworm had the head and front legs of a cat, but the body of a long worm. Reported from Austria, Germany and Switzerland in the 1920s, it was last 'seen' in Italy in 1954.

Many accounts of the winged serpent dragons of Wales bear a striking resemblance to the 'flying' lizards of South-East Asian forests. But how did such an exotic tropical creature reach Wales?

European dragons breathed fire and terrified people. They represented evil and the devil, unlike their Chinese counterparts who were kindly and benevolent.

St George followed the Greek and Roman heroes, fighting dragons (evil) to rescue young women (goodness). He was revered for his dragon-slaying powers. The Roman Catholic Church no longer regards him as a saint as his identity is in doubt and there have been no reports of his saintly appearance for several hundred years.

In Klagenfurt, Austria, is a dragon fountain. It was made after a lindorm's head was discovered nearby in 1335. A huge skull was found but, centuries later, it was proved to be that of a woolly rhino.

The ancient Egyptians thought that the sun god Ra would be eaten by Apep, the serpent-dragon.

It is said that, at the end of the world, an angel will cast a dragon, Satan, into a bottomless pit for a thousand years.

The giant boa-constrictors of South America could have given rise to the Aztec dragon myths.

Dragons' bones, skins, teeth, horns, brains, livers, blood, fat and saliva, were all used in Chinese medicine.

Dragons' blood was used in medieval medicine and magic. It was believed to cure kidney stones and blindness.

The gigantic fossil bones of extinct dinosaurs could have helped give rise to the legends of dragons.

The Lambton worm terrorized the village of Washington in County Durham, England, in the Middle Ages.

A monstrous sea lizard was seen in July 1915 off the Irish coast. The U-28, a German submarine, had just sunk a British ship when a huge undersea explosion blasted the creature high into the air.

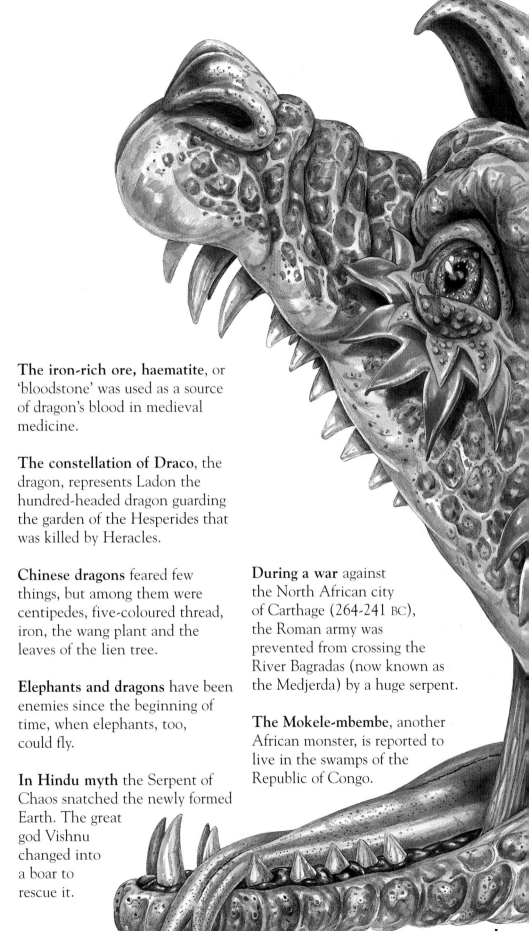

Wyverns were two-legged winged dragons. Baby wyverns look as if they would have made charming pets. But don't be deceived. The wyvern found near Mordiford, in Herefordshire, England, soon tired of saucers of milk, preferring sheep and cows instead.

King François I of France used a salamander for his royal emblem. These small dragon-like creatures were believed to survive in fire.

During the siege of Troy, the Greeks left a huge wooden horse outside the city. Sensing a trick, Laocoon, a priest of Apollo, tried to stop the Trojans taking the horse into the city. As he was doing this, two huge serpents came out of the sea and crushed him and his two sons. Interestingly, there are no large land or sea snakes in the eastern Mediterranean.

The fat from Chinese dragons could make clothes waterproof.

In ancient Norse mythology Jormungander, the Midgard serpent, encircled the earth, its huge jaws grasping its tail. Thus it will remain until Ragnarok, the Day of the Last Battle. Then it will be freed to do battle with Thor, the greatest of the Vikings' heroes.

In Hell, the demon Astaroth travels on a dragon.

The iron-rich ore, haematite, or 'bloodstone' was used as a source of dragon's blood in medieval medicine.

The constellation of Draco, the dragon, represents Ladon the hundred-headed dragon guarding the garden of the Hesperides that was killed by Heracles.

Chinese dragons feared few things, but among them were centipedes, five-coloured thread, iron, the wang plant and the leaves of the lien tree.

Elephants and dragons have been enemies since the beginning of time, when elephants, too, could fly.

In Hindu myth the Serpent of Chaos snatched the newly formed Earth. The great god Vishnu changed into a boar to rescue it.

During a war against the North African city of Carthage (264-241 BC), the Roman army was prevented from crossing the River Bagradas (now known as the Medjerda) by a huge serpent.

The Mokele-mbembe, another African monster, is reported to live in the swamps of the Republic of Congo.

Glossary

Alchemist Someone who practised alchemy (see below). The goal for most alchemists was to turn base (cheap) metals into valuable gold or silver.

Alchemy The medieval forerunner of chemistry which sought to discover how metals and other substances were made.

Anaconda The largest of the non-poisonous snakes, it kills by wrapping its muscular body around its prey and crushing it. Anacondas live in trees and rivers in South America and can grow to 9 metres in length.

Assyria A great kingdom and civilization that flourished in northern Mesopotamia (modern Iraq) from about 1950 to 600 BC, when it was defeated by the neighbouring Babylonians.

Aztec The civilization that dominated the areas of North and Central America that are now part of Mexico and Guatemala. It was overthrown by the Spanish in the 16th century.

Babylon The ancient kingdom, and its capital city, that flourished in southern Mesopotamia around 1750 to 540 BC.

Buddhism The system of religion and philosophy founded by Gautama Buddha in India in the 5th century BC.

Cockerel A male chicken. Also known as a rooster.

Dreamtime The 'golden age' in the mythology of some Australian Aboriginals when their first ancestors were created.

Etruscan The people of an ancient kingdom in central Italy. They were defeated by the Romans in the 3rd century BC and became part of the Roman Empire.

Gaudi, Antonio (1852-1926) Renowned Spanish architect. Although unfinished, the Sagrada Familia in Barcelona, Spain, is probably his most famous building.

Hinduism The main religion of India and one of the world's oldest religions.

Islam The religion of Muslims based on the teachings of the Prophet Muhammad (who died in AD 632) as set out in the Qur'an.

Maya The civilization that developed in what are now southern Mexico, Honduras, Guatemala and the Yucatan Peninsula of Central America. It was at its height between about AD 400 and 800.

Mesopotamia The area between the rivers Tigris and Euphrates (now in Iraq) where the great early civilizations of Assyria and Babylon flourished from about 1950 to 540 BC.

Metamorphose To change form.

Old Testament The first 39 books of the Christian Bible. The first five of these books also form the basis of Jewish law and beliefs.

Oriental Something relating to one of the eastern civilizations.

Pitch A dark sticky substance obtained from tar. It is semi-liquid when hot, but solidifies as it cools.

Python In mythology the huge serpent killed by Apollo at Delphi. In real life a large non-poisonous constricting snake (like the anaconda) that lives in forests and rivers in Africa and India.

Sage A very wise person.

Taoism Chinese religion and philosophy based on the writings of Laoze (sometimes called Lao-tzu) who lived around 500 BC.

Toltecs The people who lived in Mexico before the Aztecs. The Aztecs overthrew their kingdom in the 12th century.

Valley of the Queens The burial place of many of the wives and daughters of the pharaohs of ancient Egypt.

Wattle The loose, fleshy growth on the head and below the beak of turkeys and cockerels (also known as roosters).

Index

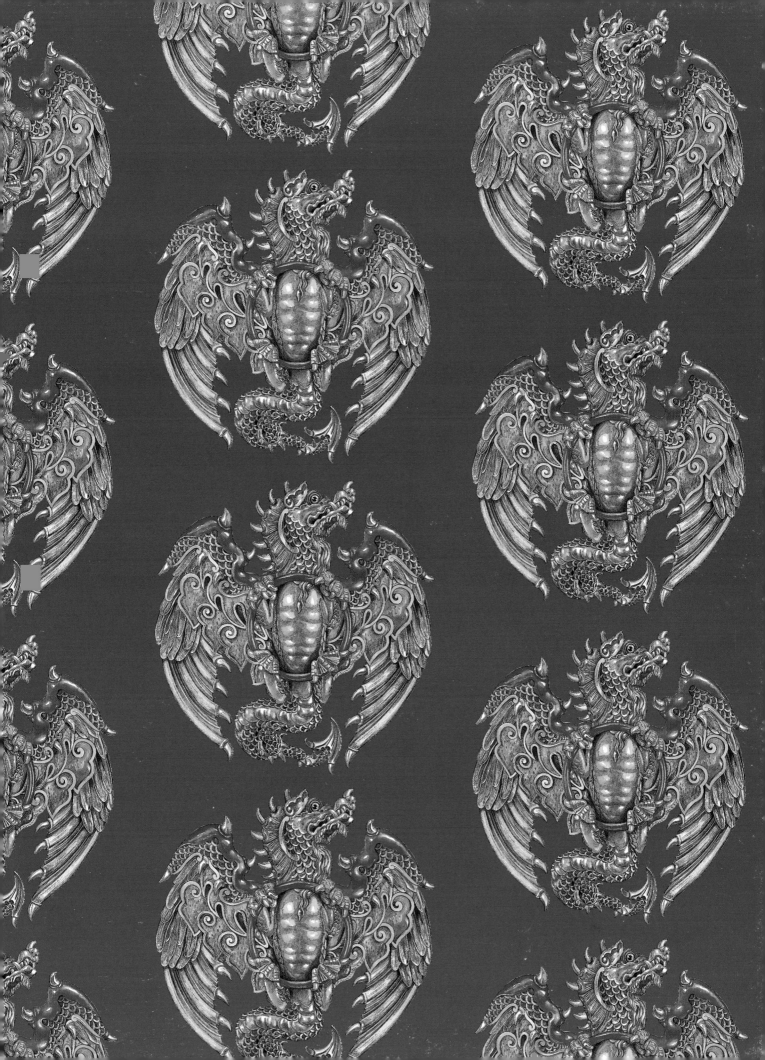